DRAGONS

Thanks to our adviser for her expertise, research, and advice:
Elizabeth Tucker, PhD.
Distinguished Service Professor
English, General Literature and Rhetoric
Binghamton University, Binghamton, NY

Editor: Shelly Lyons
Designer: Hilary Wacholz
Art Director: Kay Fraser
Production Specialist: Kathy McColley

Picture Window Books are published by Capstone
1710 Roe Crest Drive, North Mankato, Minnesota 56003
www.capstonepub.com

Library of Congress Cataloging-in-Publication Data
Names: Doeden, Matt, author. Title: Dragons / by Matt Doeden.
Description: North Mankato, MN : Picture Window Books, 2019. | Series: Mythical
creatures | Audience: Age 5-7. | Audience: K to grade 3. Identifiers: LCCN 2019004854|
ISBN 9781515844433 (hardcover) | ISBN 9781515844471 (ebook pdf)
Subjects: LCSH: Dragons—Juvenile literature. Classification: LCC GR830.D7 D643
2019 | DDC 398.24/54—dc23 LC record available at https://lccn.loc.gov/2019004854

All internet sites appearing in back matter were available and accurate
when this book was sent to press.

Printed and bound in the USA.

PA71

DRAGONS

BY
MATT DOEDEN

ILLUSTRATED BY
MARTIN BUSTAMANTE

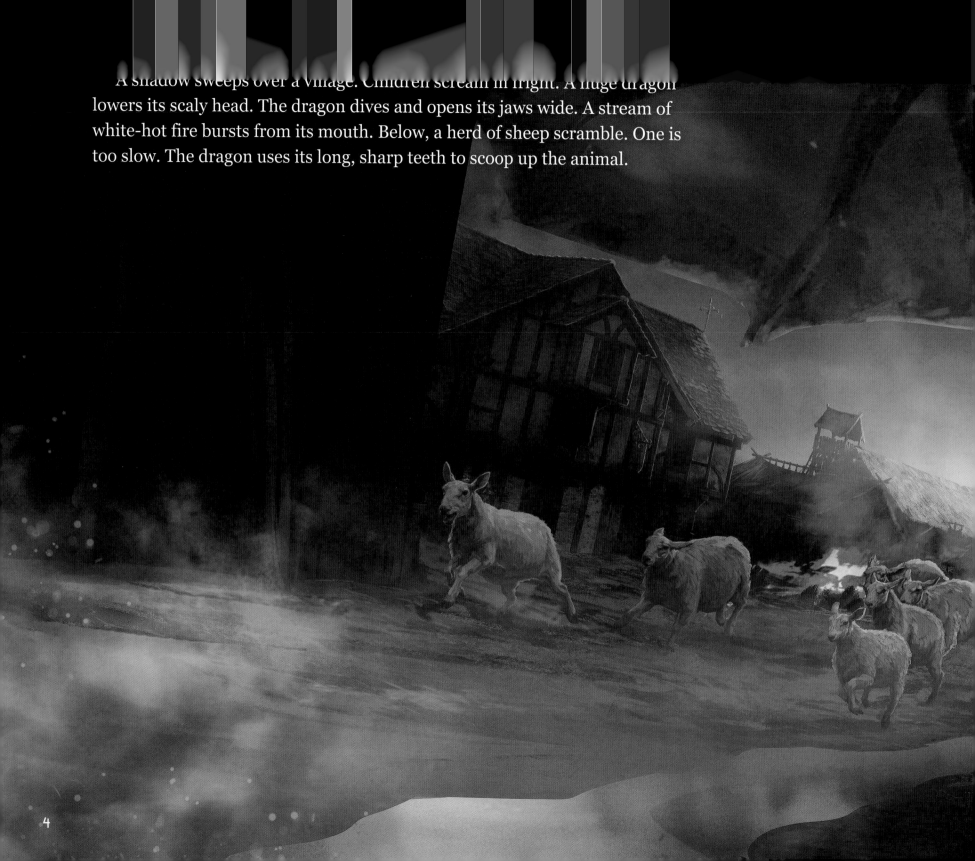

A shadow sweeps over a village. Children scream in fright. A huge dragon lowers its scaly head. The dragon dives and opens its jaws wide. A stream of white-hot fire bursts from its mouth. Below, a herd of sheep scramble. One is too slow. The dragon uses its long, sharp teeth to scoop up the animal.

4

DRAGON BEHAVIOR

Dragons are mysterious. People don't know a lot about their lives. Every dragon begins life in an egg. Female dragons lay their eggs in lairs. Dragon mothers care for their hatchlings until they're able to fend for themselves.

Young dragons must leave the nest to find their own lairs. Most dragon lairs are deep inside caves. Dragons collect treasure and keep their hoards inside the lair.

Dragons are carnivores. They hunt for meat. Young dragons seek out small prey such as mice. As dragons grow, they hunt bigger prey. Adult dragons can eat a cow or buffalo in a single meal!

LIFE CYCLE OF A DRAGON

Adult dragons may sleep for weeks or even years at a time. They wake to hunt, collect treasure, and mate. The older a dragon is, the more it sleeps.

EGG

HATCHLING

YOUNG DRAGON

Knights and other dragon slayers kill some dragons. But most dragons have very long lives. They may live for hundreds or even thousands of years. Some believe these great beasts can live forever. They may remain deep in their lairs, sleeping away the centuries!

ADULT DRAGON

ANCIENT DRAGON

DRAGON FEATURES

Dragons come in a variety of shapes and sizes. Dragons from Western legends tend to be large, but dragons from Eastern legends are often small. Most dragons, large or small, share a few common features. Dragons look like serpents or lizards. They are long and slender. Their bodies are covered with hard scales. The beasts' tough scales protect them from all but the sharpest weapons.

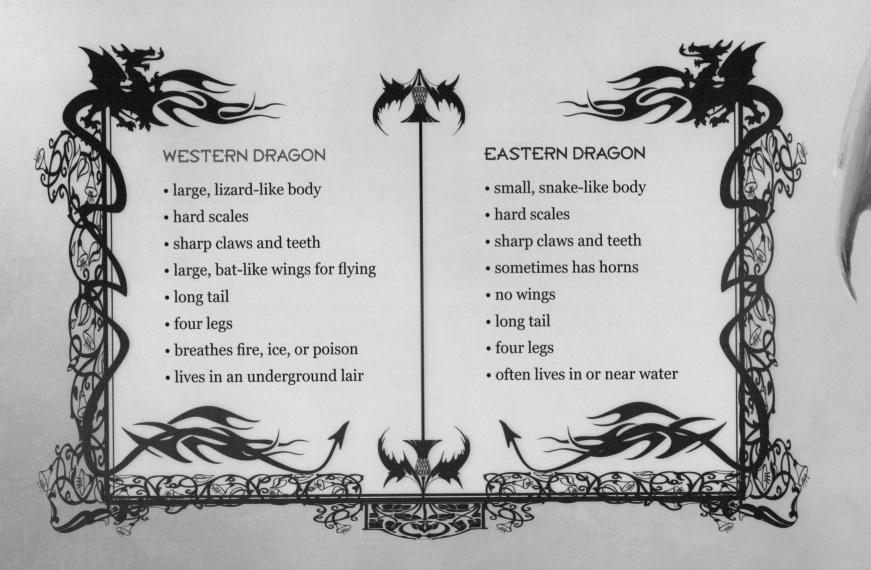

WESTERN DRAGON

- large, lizard-like body
- hard scales
- sharp claws and teeth
- large, bat-like wings for flying
- long tail
- four legs
- breathes fire, ice, or poison
- lives in an underground lair

EASTERN DRAGON

- small, snake-like body
- hard scales
- sharp claws and teeth
- sometimes has horns
- no wings
- long tail
- four legs
- often lives in or near water

EASTERN DRAGON

WESTERN DRAGON

13

Most dragons have wings. They are large and leathery.
They look like the wings of a bat.

ARMS

A dragon's arms are strong
enough to flap large wings.

METACARPALS

Like a human and a bat, a dragon has five
metacarpals on each arm. These "fingers"
make up the bones in each wing.

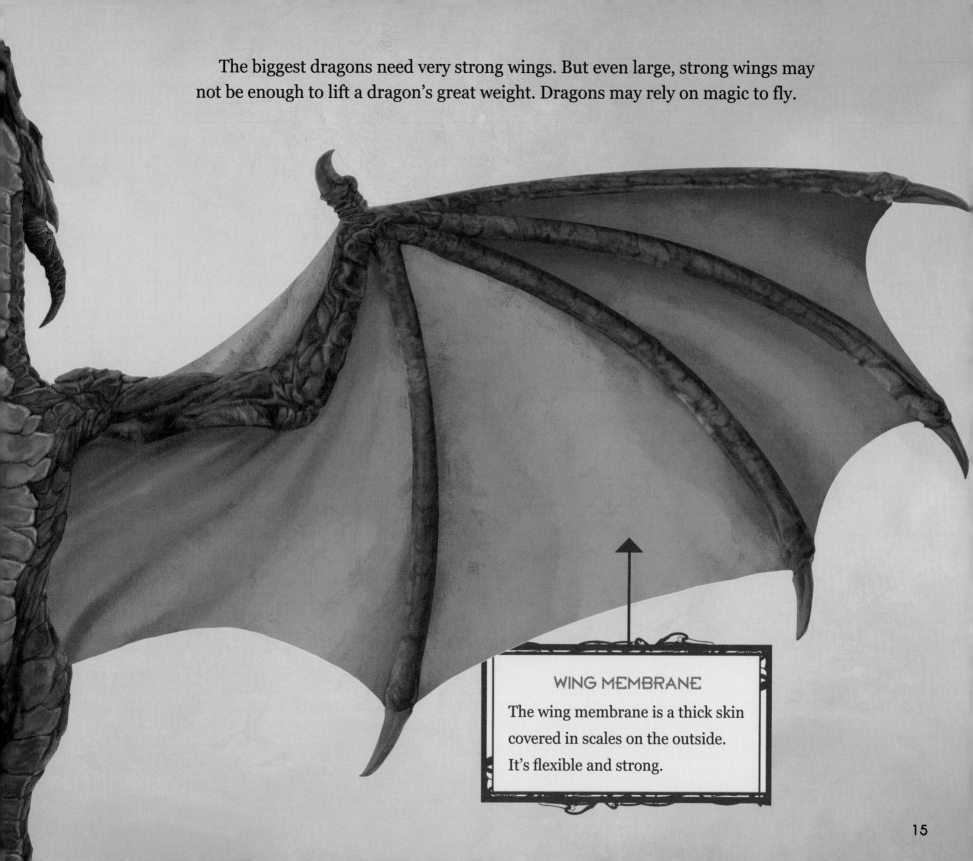

The biggest dragons need very strong wings. But even large, strong wings may not be enough to lift a dragon's great weight. Dragons may rely on magic to fly.

WING MEMBRANE

The wing membrane is a thick skin covered in scales on the outside. It's flexible and strong.

A dragon can be deadly. Its sharp teeth can rip apart any animal—or enemy. Its claws sink deep into the flesh of its prey.

A dragon can also use its tail as a weapon. A powerful whip of the tail can crush a knight's armor.

When a dragon opens its mouth, it's time to run!

Many dragons can breathe fire. But fire isn't the only kind of dragon breath. Some dragons breathe blasts of ice. Others spew deadly poison.

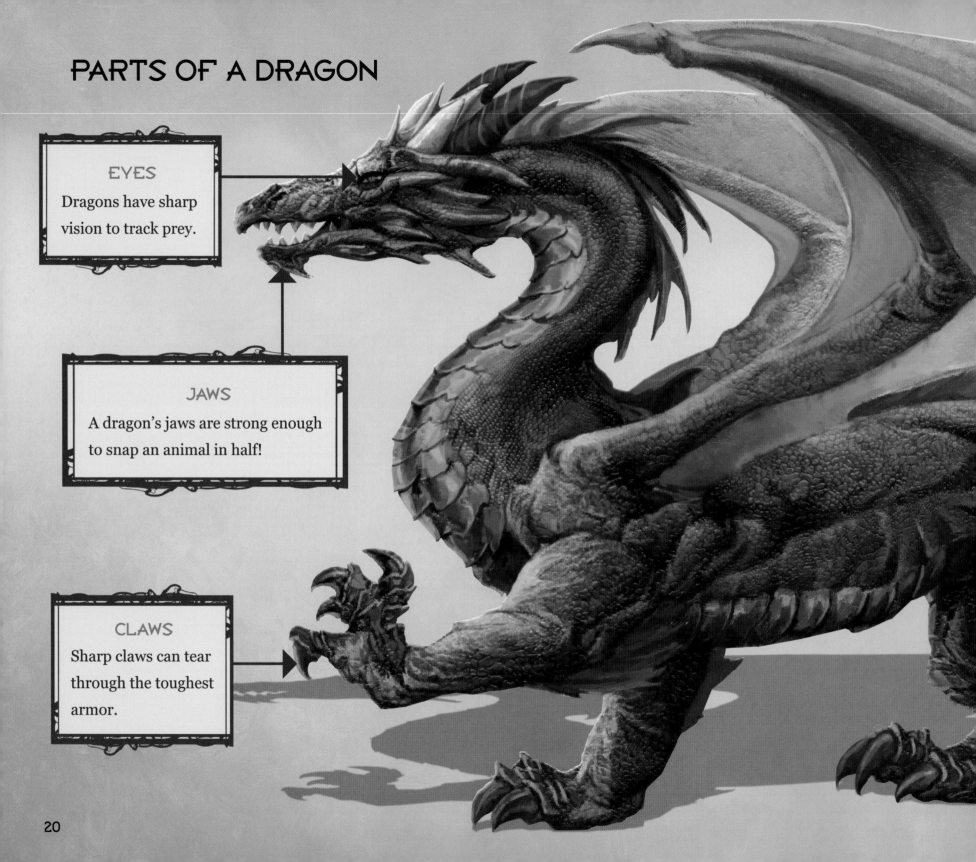

PARTS OF A DRAGON

EYES

Dragons have sharp vision to track prey.

JAWS

A dragon's jaws are strong enough to snap an animal in half!

CLAWS

Sharp claws can tear through the toughest armor.

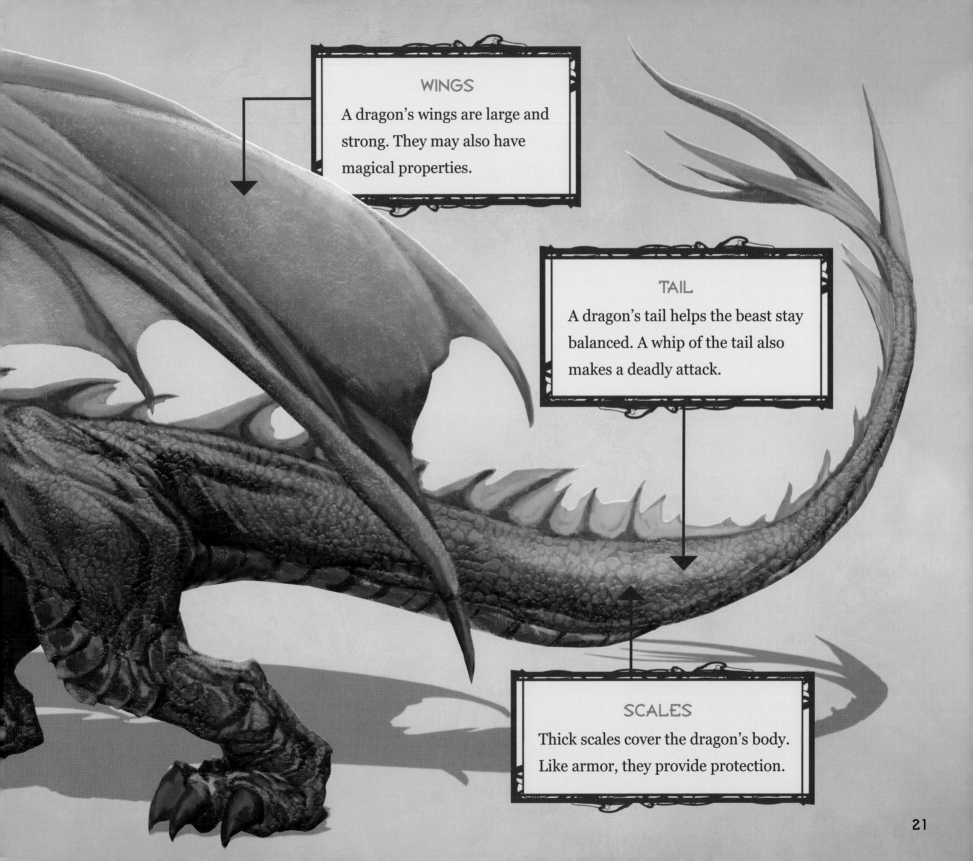

WINGS

A dragon's wings are large and strong. They may also have magical properties.

TAIL

A dragon's tail helps the beast stay balanced. A whip of the tail also makes a deadly attack.

SCALES

Thick scales cover the dragon's body. Like armor, they provide protection.

DRAGONS OF MYTH

Dragons are beasts of myth. People have told stories of these great creatures for thousands of years. Many dragons are frightful. Tiamat was a dragon goddess in stories from ancient Babylon. She gathered other dragons and monsters to fight against gods.

The story of Fafnir comes from northern Europe. Fafnir was a man who turned into a dragon. He guarded his treasure with breath of poison.

Other dragons are helpful. Chinese legend tells of the four dragons. They gave the land its rivers. They are the Black Dragon, the Long Dragon, the Pearl Dragon, and the Yellow Dragon. "The Dragon's Pearl," another Chinese legend, tells of a dragon that gave a man a pearl. The pearl gave

Dragons are still a big part of myths and legends today. Stories and movies show them as wise, powerful, and mysterious. The dragon Smaug in the beloved book *The Hobbit*, by J.R.R. Tolkien, terrorized the land.

Dragons are also part of many games. Video game players ride and slay dragons. Players in the game *Dungeons and Dragons* hunt dragons and collect treasure.

ABOUT THE AUTHOR

Matt Doeden began his career as a sportswriter. Since then he's spent almost two decades writing and editing hundreds of children's fiction and nonfiction books. *Darkness Everywhere: The Assassination of Mohandas Gandhi* was listed among 2014's Best Children's Books of the Year from the Children's Book Committee at the Bank Street College of Education. Doeden lives in Minnesota with his wife and two children.

ABOUT THE ILLUSTRATOR

Martin Bustamante is an illustrator and painter from Argentina. At the age of three he was able to draw a horse "starting by the tail", as his mother always says. As a teenager, he found in movies like *Star Wars* and books like *Prince Valiant,* by Harold Foster, new and fascinating worlds full of colors, shapes, and atmospheres that became his inspiration for drawing. He started working as a professional illustrator and has worked for several editorials and magazines, from Argentina to the United States to Europe.

GLOSSARY

ancient—from a long time ago

carnivore—an animal that eats only meat

century—a period of 100 years

hatchling—a recently hatched animal

hoard—money or other valuables that are stored or hidden away

knight—a warrior of the Middle Ages (AD 400–1500) who wore armor and usually fought on horseback

lair—a dragon's home, often hidden deep underground

myth—a traditional story, often from ancient times

poison—a substance that can kill or harm someone

prey—an animal that is hunted by another animal for food

scale—one of many small, hard pieces of skin that cover an animal's body

slay—to kill

spew—to spit or spray with great force

CRITICAL THINKING QUESTIONS

1. Dragon myths come from all around the world. Do you think the idea of dragons is common?

2. Dragons from ancient China and the Eastern world tend to be helpful. Those from Europe and the Western world tend to be harmful. Why might this be true?

3. Some experts think dragon legends are related to people's experiences with huge snakes and dinosaur fossils. What do you think they might be related to?

READ MORE

Loh-Hagan, Virginia. *Dragons: Magic, Myth, and Mystery*. Magic, Myth, and Mystery. Ann Arbor: Cherry Lake Publishing, 2017.

Marsico, Katie. *Beastly Monsters: From Dragons to Griffins*. Monster Mania. Minneapolis: Lerner Publications, 2017.

Sautter, A.J. *Discover Dragons, Giants, and Other Deadly Fantasy Monsters*. All About Fantasy Creatures. North Mankato, MN: Capstone Press, 2018.

INTERNET SITES

Kids Play and Create
https://www.kidsplayandcreate.com/do-dragons-breathe-fire-fun-dragon-facts-for-kids/

Ducksters: Ancient China Mythology
https://www.ducksters.com/history/china/chinese_mythology.php

UNICORNS

by Cari Meister
illustrated by Daniel Whisker

MERMAIDS

by Cari Meister
illustrated by Xavier Bonet

DRAGONS

by Matt Doeden
illustrated by Martin Bustamante

GRIFFINS

BY MATT DOEDEN
ILLUSTRATED BY MARTIN BUSTAMANTE